THE LONG GAP

ANTHONY KELLMAN

PEEPAL TREE

First published in Great Britain in 1996
Peepal Tree Press Ltd
17 King's Avenue
Leeds LS6 1QS

ISBN 0 948833 78 5

For Malaika

ACKNOWLEDGEMENTS

Acknowledgement is made to the editors of the following magazines in which some of these poems first appeared:

Black Buzzard Review for 'Another Wave';*Chelsea* for 'Fishing Song'; *Graham House Review* for 'Isle Man,' and 'Graves of the Sea'; *Kyk-Over-Al (Guyana)* for 'Island Lover' and 'Hinckson'; *Obsidian 11* for 'Conversation With a Dead Politician (or Shak-Shak)', 'Summer Heat', and 'Creatures'; *Poetry Review* (London) for 'Airport Revisited' and 'A Churn in the South'; *The Literary Half-Yearly* (India) for 'Wharf Story', 'Ballad of the Limestone', and 'Freedom Man'; *Visions International* for 'Somewhere, Somewhere'.

These poems were written with the support of the National Endowment for the Arts

CONTENTS

FISHING SONG

MORNING

I watch dem. I watch dem ev'ry single morning
come here to wo'k: de Bajan fishermen.
Their journey ain't easy, but still they carry on:
The seas may be rough, but there's always a rising sun.
I watch dem, I watch dem ev'ry single morning
come here to wo'k: de Bajan fishermen.

Another light.
A moses, black and green hyphen, squats
on the edge of the earth.
A fisherman and his mate grab it
like every man his morsel. It eats
through the sand like a lion fish
and bores into its blue rest.

Up the beach, in the distance,
the fisherman's wife leaps into the light
twin buckets syncopating
with remnants of yesterday's catch.
She skips, in accurate dactyls,
with her coin-tinkling apron,
her newspaper wraps and plastic bags
and her raw love. She is coming toward me,
out of reach of hotels sprawled in concrete,
through the thorn-shrouded furnaces
of bougainvillaea.

"Feeeeeesh...feeeesh. Get your feeeesh!
Four for a dollar!"

My nirvana hisses like foam, like fossil,
on the blazing sand dunes at this Brighton.
Her rainbow skirt swirls
in the heart of the sun.

"Feeesh... feeesh...Get your fresh feesh!
Four for a dollar!"

Once, I moved myself far from here,
far from this provincial earth
which, now, I am shouldering again.
I devour her braid-dripping head crowned with straw.
I stuff myself with her rainbows.
Please trust me. I am not the enemy.
It's here, in this salt-caked workshop,
I learnt to throw a line. Like you,
my only loyalty was surf. But that
wasn't enough for the blacker than blacks.
So I sailed north on a raft of almond leaves,
heaving and calm, lean and glorious,
oyster among lions...

The moses, an outcast but independent sperm,
wriggles on to the horizon.
The raged hand hurls its dynamite
and the sea explodes.

MIDDAY

Music is a woman that I love;
she does give me de food I eat.
Music is a woman that I need,
'cause she does give me all the air that I breathe.

Music is a woman that I love,
'cause she does give me de food I eat.
I said. music is a woman that I need,
'cause she does give me all de air that I breathe.

My body clang-out like a cymbal.
Wha' part I goin' go?
Wha' part I goin' run
from this sun?
I ten miles 'pon top Atlantis third heaven.
And me woman?
She just come in from massaging de earth
after two whole hours.

I cast I net and I wait, rocking with surf music.
I nod I head and I wait and hold on tight to me rod.
In de four-room chattel, the two boychile out to school,
me woman alone shellin' green peas in de lap o' she apron.
And she size-up de swell-up husks, scoop-out de seeds
and, easy so, toss de empty shells down on de crocus bag
spread out like a raft in front she.
And she sing and sing and sing:

"Music is a good man that I love,
'cause he does give me de food I eat.
Music is a good man that I need,
'cause he does give me all de air that I breathe."

And then she whistle a whistle, a long real sweet whistle
and de sound of the husks in de grooves of the raft
is a drum-beat to she lips,
is a chord-twang from off o' she lips.

EVENING

Crimson, yellow, orange, purple splash
an' dance on de sky fade-up blue jeans.
And everything good.
De sun weary but everything good.
De moses, bulging wid garfish, snapper, seacat, cavali,
nose-in 'pon de pebbly shore.
The children home from school
(without bruises, praise de Lord).
The kitchen pregnant with fried dolphin.

When we finish eating at we table,
the deal-board table which you mek wid you own hands,
the boys goin' go out to play with them friends,
and then we go put-on some music 'pon de stereo,
and, Big Man, um is me and you alone in here.
Big Man, um is me and you and a big-able bed.

It's a long time, Man, me never feel you,
Come, let me hold your hand.
It's a long time, Man, me never feel you,
Come, let me hold your hand.

We can't escape this rhythm.
We can't escape the blessing.
Whatever we do, we remember, we remember,
we remember we is de music; we remember,
we remember, we remember we is de music.
Reggae, ruk-a-tuk, samba, calypso: all of it is we music,
throbbing there in your big-big biceps,
shining in the Caribbean moon.

Caribbean moon, yellow yellow
Caribbean moon, yellow yellow
Caribbean moon, yellow yellow
Caribbean moon shine all night.

BALLAD OF THE LIMESTONE

Nelson is a monolith,
hand-clutched pistol raised to God.
Over the cityscape, he lifts
his larvae-breeding rod.

Vexed in bronze, eyes pinned to the sky,
Bussa breaks the island's heart.
Pitying one's own pedigree
is a mental wart.

Had not for that black lighting,
chains would have howled another night,
and Independence would have thinned
and leaked its light.

On an eastern coast, saltwater
eats a castle's legs.
Bussa fighting still. My daughter
will see the ramparts fall, the dregs

of its symbol dissolved in salt:
new reefs, new fish,
no sirens of lanterns, no fault
of history glaring through coconut ribs.

So a man, hobbling,
spools his net of words.
Vowels skip and sing;
some glide like seabirds.

Year after year, patient in craft,
as parties come and go,
his lines work like a laugh
of fingers on a fret board.

In the scat of a guitar strum,
a rebel's breath is caught.
An El Verno del Congo drum
sounds between two thoughts.

Lines and spaces, bird and breath,
converge around this altar
of limestone. What's left
is heroic. Unaging star.

CREATURES

I see it! Look it there! Ears pricked like a Doberman's.
Snake eyes. The nose, an exclamation mark,
A moving mouth. Black, staring at me
over the top of my back paling.
A tide of panic scours my insides;
my heart, a goby in a spotted moray's mouth.
It looks like the fear of invasion
has finally gotten to me.
Ever since Bishop took the bullet of betrayal,
everywhere you turn, in every island heart and vein,
conquistadorial morality.
Khus-khus hedges tremble.
Breadfruits hang like oversized hand grenades.
I tell you, it's all so upsetting.
Only last week, a boasting CBC
saw an unidentified creature coasting south.
Turned out to be a light
amphibious plane,
from a U.S. film company,
examining a site
for a feature film on
terrorism.

I rub my eyes with the fury of the ixora,
but the creature's stare keeps piercing me.
I stare back, still and waiting, locked
in the creature's waiting eyes.
Blackbirds and wood doves hop in and out
of mahogany trees. The palms shimmy.
A bus tumbles along the nearby road.

I am Jonathan Columbus, fixed in fear.
When the forest's screaming eyes enfold me,
I set out to overcome and tame the native,

15

arrest the boiling bloods of every last Arawak and Carib.
I edge my way along time's side paling
and peep around the corner. Nothing
but the sound of the palm's howling hair
and a bellied palm branch leaning harmless ribs
on the back of the paling.

Disoriented, I return to the house. On the steps,
I look again toward my corrugated past.
The creature stares at me. Black. Moving mouth.
I start, rush forward to seize and kill
the renewing foetal fear, conquer primordial fear
setting like a stone in my stomach.
I skid as I gain the end of the paling
and strike it hard. Something falls to the ground
with a thud and I, Jonathan Carib/Jonathan Arawak, witness,
in that swift descent through times and spaces, my own
(re)living of past and future buried worlds.

I am conqueror. I am conquered.

The fallen branch had angled to show its two faces
— ageless branch and creature spirit — marrying
in one transient, eternal movement.
The curved branch had struck the ground
and laid flat on its back.
Pricked ears. An exclamation mark.
Snake eyes. The mouth, a vowel of sunlight,
spills through the eye of a mahogany tree
set in motion by an infinite breeze.

ISLE MAN

After last night's howling winds and its rivers of rain,
now pooled for any Narcissus, the fenced yard's poxed
with broken dogwood limbs and leaves
scattered like dead soldiers and their shed fatigues.
I will rake them into a November pile:
heaped thoughts crumbling in their mound.
Circling, ever-circling, this ague-shaken earth, the sound
of bluejays cheupsing acappella.
Why are you so despondent, Man?
Is it the ancestral bark of nearby century-old oaks
poised to march at Lee's exacting roar?
Is it the memory of a promise, flaked soggy leaves,
never kept: after Emancipation, forty acres and a mule?

Tonight, head on my pillow, eyes closed,
the flip-side of memory revolves
and the needle in this groove audibly details
an orange island sunset collapsing like a flag.
It is lovely in death, lovely
as the lowering of empirical red, white, and blue
one November night on the Garrison Savannah
when an island witnessed the skyward flutter
of a new broken age: a sunwashed island
wrapped with lucid blue bandages
a broken trident driven into its eye.

Ah! The whole Diaspora shakes in my skin!
My burden is great, but I am blessed.
I am blessed because saltwater heals
all manner of illness. I survive
because I can return.
And what about the rum-guzzling suitors
who desecrate the sea goddess's hut:
big-guts creatures wielding pitchforks,

hiding behind rhetoric and a big-shot laugh?
Isle Man, what about the suitors?
My words will slit their throats, gouge-out their eyes,
and saw their malice in half.

GRAVES OF THE SEA

The air I carry bubbles into globes.
I level at fifty. There's nothing I want to miss.
Underneath, the ocean floor spreads like a stingray's back.
A stream of sun rays knife softly from above.
Yards in front me, the wreck is waiting,
limbs dark, Gothic, opaque:
another version of the colonial ache.
I advance with an escort of angel fish.
I see the rusted anchor and chain. My cohorts
fin-thrill, but all my mulling thoughts
muster are pictures of sunken galleons,
once manned by the ruthless British and Spanish,
and I feel that some retribution has been earned.
I touch the chain and make a wish:
that every act of hate would partake of water
and pay their dues with earnings from the tourist dollar
and if they don't drown, then, by God, let them burn;
the fire coral, grinning in red, would see to that.
The burning crosses, swastikas, subtle insults and exclusions,
would be weighed and brought here each in their turn
where all history congeals in a sick embrace
as when maggots feast ceremoniously on a man's face
with nearby ixoras and hibiscus plants sprouting
like the multicoloured fins of fantails. Once, I strove
to hold history in my right hand. The only lack was frequency.
Now, I kiss the seabed and see Man's wreckage in all its modes.

A MINIBUS NAMED "SCORPION"

A blue and yellow insect elbows
down steaming asphalt toward me
scorpion eyes widely hypnotic
shoulders ringing with profit
and dub music.

> *I want to tell you 'bout dem young girls.*
> *They got more tricks than they got curls.*
> *Love me, love me. Will you love me?*
> Watch out!
> *Love me, love me. Will you love me?*
> Watch out!

On the back of the driver's cage:
NO SMOKING - NO NUTS - NO FREE RIDERS.
I watch the unfurling rage
of other banners, metallic, scouring the highway: "Road Warrior",
"Mafia", "First Blood", "Dreader than Dread",
"The Stars", "Her Majesty", "Not Guilty, Your Honour".
If you cross the road during this war, Brother, you dead.

Route restrictions? Stiffer license fees?
None brings the minibus men to their knees.
Survival justifies the danger,
as they cling like crabs to the tar's raging seas.

Some humid days, I myself can't take it.
Today, I'm in control. I disembark
and saunter to the guest house
casting back one nostalgic glance for which I feel no shame.
This, after all, is home My rabid peace,
my people's dance, my simple name.

In an hour, my time will be up,
and I'll be drawn away once more
from my buried navel-string
and the dialect of this sun.
Twice a year I come to speak
with my ancestors, to slake
my craving for saltwater.

ISLAND LOVER

(In Memory of A.J. Seymour)

Over white and black-washed walls,
whose hand let down the golden page?
Who set eager new stanzas crammed like canefields?
When island doors howled shut
and my frenzy scurried like dried wind-driven leaves
along limestone walkways,
who let down the golden page?

When Independence made men murder their own mothers
for a step-up, Island Lover clothed himself
with humility and the limb of a dream. He climbed
with eyes on God alone. And when I wrote "The King"
(a steep hill, an old man climbing)
his archetype ruled my hopeful hand
until flesh piled on top my book of dreams.

Life's mysteries leap
in silent confidence from my fingers:
a bearded fig tree, a curving girl garlanded
with jewels from a coral reef.

Seventy-five steps to the celestial city.
Seventy-five steps to the golden gate.
And for all this, his music of love,
his songs of ancients and the new-born,
we give thanks and praise the Good Lord.

BURN THEM

Fire roared from the vinyl of the abandoned *Ford*.
Hardly any wind. Still, precise flames darted
and licked the roof of the house.
In other northern places,
those cured flanks may have burnt,
but, down here,
where homes nudge one another,
the water hoses and buckets of sand
briskly crowded the yard.
Twelve broken glass louvers and a singed back roof,
the only damage. The little girl's
twenty-pound aquarium with its golden fantails,
her glossy red doll's house, and her walking dolls
all safe, all sound
in the cradle of mercy.

A sign? But what it mean? The sure corruption
of all temporal things? Or was I driven
by unconscious ritual lust to confront
and erase the age that mocked my youth?
Driven to flirt with fire. I was, involuntarily, driven
to behold my crumbling body in the splash
of fire: potential nightmare element
in every last one of us,
fifteen maggots on a dead man's chest.

CALYPSO'S ISLAND

(In Memory of Bruce St. John)

On a palm-spangled island
in the middle of the sea, I sigh
with the casuarina's grating threnody.
I go under the bamboo's coarse dominance
engulfed in an eternity of limbo.
"I won't feed you," Calypso said,
plebeian guts spilling over his pants.
"But take a rest and you dead."

I yearn for a different shore
to elude indigenous vines
encircling me like snakes. For years,
Calypso coaxed me with rhetoric
to turn my mind from leaving.
But the day I said, "I'll stay" and went under the pole again,
ten snakes coiled out from *his* head and whipped the air.
"I won't feed you," Calypso hissed. "Eat my words instead.
But take a rest and you dead."

Through tenebrous back alleys
choked with crack and rum,
a fine actor scuttles. A poet's
filed and forgotten in some
sweltering Government office, silenced
by paperwork. A painter changes his palette
for a calypso, entitled, "Ah want to whine
and jam a woman tonight".

Will I join them, or will I accept
a foreign hand and earn a living from my art?
A wound opens wide inside me,
for where shall a man find sweetness
to surpass that of his own home?

After heroic waters and the bitter cup,
my back-bone snaps under the ever-lowering rod,
and I become a shadow on the sea's rim
as those who've gone before
      impalpable
      wavering
yearning for some other ground
but kissing the one I'm on.

SEA HORSE, PASS BY

(In memory of Timothy Callender)

1

A mare, water like broken mirrors falling from its sides,
erupts from the depths, bares its teeth, neighs.
Tongues of water lick its grey body.
How long had it been there, this disturbed quadruped
hidden by water bodies, water shields?
Why wasn't it affected this way before?
Why this precise moment?
Did it suddenly sense a grotesque spirit,
a bent and pathetic twisting creature?

The spirit sensed by the animal is mine.
When it hoisted itself and powerfully neighed,
the forcefields dissolved in surf
and, by accident of water, I confronted it.

Was it also a demonic apparition?
A male beast in female form?
Should I drown myself and be rid
of its hellish haunt and nightmare of values?
Values. Morality. I no longer know the meaning
of such words. I want release. Release!
The androgynous mirror crushes me
though it never moves an inch, teeth bared
in a clownish laugh: grotesque,
condemnatory, derisive laugh.

Drawing back, I nose-dive into the depths of this age,
eyes eating for the light of a sea cellar door.
I angle my head towards the water-softened sun
still mighty up there, throwing crystal fragments
that light the seabed and my impotent ecstasy.

26

My lungs empty of air.
Not a single inlet to be found.
A patch of moss reaches out its tentacles,
binds me, and I inhale, with agitated pleasure,
the saltwater kingdoms of my tribe.

2

Teachers said I had a talent for words,
and, before challenging the Beast, I was a local star.
Integrity demands every soul's day of resistance
(O truth! O Mandela! O righteous war!)

So I lost membership with the partisan class,
became a manuscript stencilled and filed in St. George.
More than half my life I laboured with words, canvas;
yet, the job I most suited was offered

to a stranger with no experience in the field.
The convenient reason for a favour given?
"Cally is a artist, and you know how they are.
They walk in air and contemplate the sun."

So I left it all, left it all,
left those floors fouled by institutional serfs.
Now each day I respond to the sea's call
and wrap my burdens in surf.

3

Lungs bursting with the brimstone of the sea,
what tide now releases me
so that I flying-fish to the surface
endlessly gasping?

The creature still stands with its clownish grin.
A mat of tangled seaweed breaks the shining surface.
A black muscular body follows it. The rasta
loudly blows his nose, wipes water from his face,
flicks his terrible locks.
Like fluttering leaves, they shake dry.

Though I realise that sentence has already been passed,
I know I have tamed the four-footed beast
(two of its own; two of a political party).
I lay-float and, for the first time,
contemplate the sun.
High up there, in all that blue loveliness,
I see my spirit and know my stare
won't redirect it to my body.
The leavening glare doesn't even make me blink.
I am no longer afraid, no longer deprived.
I see my grave in the sky.

ALL O' WE IS ONE

Welcome, one and all, to Crop Over Festival,
music playing, listen to de bass.
It is bacchanal in de place,
men and women whining up their waists...

—Traveller

Late-July, de Crop Over fever soar
so high the only thing could cure
it is de Kadooment sweat-let. Early morning costume
bands gather like armies at the Stadium. Tune
most played in de parade and the non-stop
jump-up to Spring Garden take prize for Pic-o-de-Crop.
First out is 'The War Lords', splendorous in heat,
followed by Jordan's 'Jumby Jamboree'.
The sequinned devils raise pitchforks and prance like shite
round de Stadium; stands pack like for a Tyson fight.
Marcia Blackman come out wid 'Pride and Industry',
praising de country for opportunity
to let all o' we let-off last year's steam.
They jump up and wo'k-up bad; confetti faces gleam.
The road to Spring Garden ring wid all kind o' people:
young, old, rich, poor, islander, tourist. Pull
of the crowd is a river gone wild,
Drink stalls, hemming the highway, make a fortune, child!
In de rum and de sun and de bacchanal,
costumes, crafted for months, will fall from the festival.
After the howl of that sweat
be towelled off, we all forget.
When Kadooment Day gone with a toss,
the highways clean up and masks come off.
Who'll hear that stall operator who food we just taste?
Who'll remember her face?

WHARF STORY

Once upon a time, and not so long ago,
I saw Bajan boys, fig-navelled, snotty-nosed,
gathering by the Bridgetown Wharf. Already rehearsed,

they wait in gaping shirts and pants,
shoeless and with knitted faces.
Foreign cameras, coins, and faces

advance towards the city. Rum-flushed, sun-burnt,
in rainbow shorts the visitors hurl pennies into the dark
current and await the water's howl.

They applaud (as boys bore like fantails
into the depths), and chatter like *Challenger's* crowd
when two minutes pass. What if the experiment fails?

Soon, black hands puncture the surface; each raised trophy
acknowledged with a din. Jerked by that roar, a straw hat sails
into the murk. A fat man bellows: "Boy, get my hat for me!'

The memory throbs with shame. Today, we are seduced
by a dawn that hymns a subtler story.
The conquistador slides inside our skin! He's reproduced

inside brick houses that mottle the heights and terraces,
a black man bellowing at his own, a black
child deaf to the strum of ancestral glory.

THE LAST STRONGHOLD
(for Hilary Beckles)

Last evening, in the congealing darkness,
after kissing my son goodnight,
after escaping domestic sights that can wrench
the revolutionary hand, I calmly turned again
page after painful page of our economic history.
The indigenous leaves lengthen like caneblades.
Through the ribs of coconut trees, I heard
ancestral voices, insistent as waves, humming, "Justice",
and I knew my mouth could not be stopped.

This morning, Mary's brow drips question marks.
I tell her what my conscience said
and how those voices aroused in me
each subterranean pool and leaf and river.
She squeezes my hand and I advance
towards the white-washed monolith.

Ears ringing with death-threats, I push
against time-honoured barriers of privilege and power
that cast long white shadows over this land
and I know there can be no crumbling,
no dissolution of economic unfairness,
without the march and the conchshell sound.

I tore the mask from the face of that beast,
revealed its true identity to the world.
Yet, my friends, it is breathing still.
Slavering, it stumbles over limestone,
contemptuous to the native drumbeat.
Now it squats on the island's shoulder.
It stares through the windows of this rock.

CONVERSATION WITH A DEAD POLITICIAN
(or SHAK-SHAK)

Then Genevieve did something she had never done before.
— *F.A Hoyos,* **Tom Adams: A Biography**

The shadow of the sun followed the sun.
Then you, the shadow, broke at the seams
and the maggots sexed in peace.
Behind your inherited beaming wit,
a seed of darkness glinted (the spoilt child's dance)
when we turned you on
in our living rooms on Budget Day,
your reeded voice smooth and low as any *Smirnoff* ad.
We smelt your *Machiavelli* through the screen!
Your heart danced on your tongue!
It shone through your eyes!

Our love was a land gulping every inch of water,
and when the seam broke and the cocaine crawled
across the island's screen, the c.i.a projected
your image on our minds and we wanted to stare away
because your father, old Sir Grantley, was such a good man.
An ox was strapped to everyone's tongue – the journalists,
even the Opposition, and the police (especially the police).
Your friend, the Syrian Mr. Guzman, charged for possession;
O the fever broke but only to rise higher. The Police rasped:
'Me hands tied. Me hands tied. O me hands tied up.'

Next week, Genevieve, whose hand you took on British soil,
did something she had never done before: after lunch,
she unfurled her silent demure beauty
toward the city to shop
while, alone, you fell to the bedroom floor,
sprawled on your back,
clutching your prized album of stamps.

No autopsy. No investigation.

The nation tortured its face into a smile.
I didn't even hear one palm tree mourn. Did you...?
Did the c.i.a...? Did a jealous lover...?
Did Castro, remembering Grenada...?
Did Genevieve...?

EVERY MAN'S GULF

1

Indigenous furies, razored with death,
snort around a rum-hot coast.
Scything over the land, they slice
the heads off palm trees clean.
I quiver north on water,
away from faceless palms,
away from the quarrelsome sea
and this sky's interminable lament.

Now, on another soil,
I'm four hours drive from the historic coast
where those cutting winds find their grave.
February. The day clear. A light wind.
Still, I think of hurricanes
and permanently decapitated palms
fringing an island's lapping shores,
stabbing the sky like wireless utility poles.

We gather our live minnows and shrimp
from a small convenience store: four men,
two generations, two cultures, yenned
to our especial patriarchy.
Wrapped in a 1978 *Malibu*,
we head south from New Orleans,
the *Glassmaster* tailing our dreams,
Japanese outboard pinned to its rear-end.

2

HIGH RIDGE MARINA
Bait — Live minnows
WELCOME TO
HIGH RIDGE

An electronic crane with two canvas straps
hoist the *Glassmaster* up and over
into the murky water. Best wishes from our hosts.
Through a galaxy of froth and a veil of engine smoke,
I see the marina and its operators fade like ghosts.
Bayous, passes, and inlets twist about us
bounded by peninsular clusters and clumps.
Fast-growing palmettoes cover
rises of sand and earth. The waterway claps.
We gorge on the cool air until we feel we'd choke.

Delicately white, still as bone china, cranes pose
on the water; awake or asleep, I cannot tell.
Hundreds more waltz in the sky: silver confetti
generously sprinkled from another world, another life.
They wink and mingle with yellow buoys
and the occasional dory with its sculptured crew,
silent as still-lives.
The pelicans, too, seem frozen to their posts,
guarding the Gulf.

We let our anchor down, thread our lives to our rods,
weight them, attach minnows to our dangerous question marks,
spool our past into the sea,
past hooks that have followed us here.
You, who drove us, raised your wife's pressure
until she died and your lover got the ring.
You, next to him, loosed your productive sex
on the outside, twice, to prove you were the head
of your house. Next to me, my contemporary
who impregnated his religious wife before marrying
and must bear the stare of her spite forever.
And I, netted with guilt for fleeing north
and leaving the scattered fronds of palms
to hum sorrowful calypsos
on the lapping shores.

A water tanker plunges from its pole perch
and bores, sword-like, five feet deep.
It arrows upward ten feet away,
its beak ribboned with a small flounder.
Three lines feel the bite.
Far beyond, death-still in the fading sun,
Grand Isle, and, behind it, the fishing camps
sprinkled like Amerindian huts on the water.
Three lines feel the bite.
Another line feels the bite.
Our families are waiting for us.
I reach over to the large red cooler.
I turn back the lid.
Five redfish, two sheephead.
One redfish, eyelight dimming with the sun,
slaps itself against a half-full bottle of rum.

FREEDOM MAN

At Techwood Drive, there's no need
to ask crispy-uniformed lawmen
the way to Bobby Dodd Stadium.
I follow the highway of people
increasing each second like sand.
Vendors hedge the road
faces beaming free enterprise:
T-shirts, pin buttons, earrings,
beads, flags in lucid blacks,
greens and yellows, the ANC's sunrise
glowing since 1912 for South Africa's oppressed.
It colours me in this June 27th Atlanta heat,
and I wait for my gate to open.

50,405 others are waiting as well
to see the one who walked into the sunlight
after twenty-seven years in thrall,
his intellect glittering still,
his will a mahogany tree guarding
the martyred graves of MLK and X,
of Bussa, Biko, and the islander,
Clement Payne, who made a ruling class get vexed...

Inside the humming arena, I find my row.
Coerced by humidity, I drink the sodas of apartheid
weeping with those who weep.

From my panoramic view where *C&S* and *Bell*
scrape the sky, I hear the performers far below:
Peabo Bryson's syrupy ballads float upward like balloons,
Third World's raunchy dub refrains
and Masekela's jubilant trumpet
are all Africa in my blood.

Above, helicopters circle endlessly
propeller-thrilled with strategies
like the SWATS positioned on roof-tops.

I see them between the buildings:
police escorts gathering like fireflies,
blue and red lights flickering.
A continent of birds flurry high up here,
agitated by history, as
all 50,406 of us stand and shout:
"Mandela! Mandela! Mandela!"

FAMILY

That Jewish gent surrounded by the vacuity of the Bronx,
is as much an islander as the man playing beach cricket
on an almond-ringed beach in Barbados!
A painting, first and foremost, is an island.
Its creator's insides inhabit it
like polyps, controlled, infinitely free.
It is framed with sand to match its colour.
It is encircled by the wall's trundling surf.
He's wise who ploughs diligently on his own turf
with silent cunning and knows it by heart,
knows the plurality sprouting from that ground:
the spaces of light, Rosen! The spaces of light around
a subject's inchoate head.
I am led like Odysseus into your protean space.
Your waterway yawns for the entrance of my bark.
There are Marlborough's children couched and tearful,
the matriarch's love holding those pebbles at the centre,
the man's right leg angled with indifference.
Once, I saw a woman rise from the sea and dance on a wave.
All areas of light grew in her hair.
The light twisted and sang.
Your matriarch reminded me of her,
so I put my face inside yours
and feel the terrible wholeness.

HINCKSON

Faithfully, Hinckson shuffles each afternoon
to the college pool where he knows there's room
for him. Schooled here, he witnessed the pressures
of Depression. Who can deprive him now of simple pleasures?
Wrinkled beyond three score and ten,
he first spoke to me in the men's locker: "When
the Sea Islanders came, they spoke just like you...
Gul... lah, Africa, Yoru..."
He raises a forefinger, doubtfully, to his lips.
"It's BAR... BARbados you're from... isn't it?"
He said black folks taught him how to speak.
As a child, he spent more time at nanny's feet
than in his own mother's arms. But now
he has difficulty fitting things he used to know.
Now, his last memories are his first.
And I look at him and my heart feels to burst.
What did he think of MLK's death?
Of desegregation? Of the racism that's left?
What were his feelings on the Civil Rights Act?
Somehow, I couldn't bring myself to ask.
He stood there painfully ordering his thoughts,
his feet shuffling with afterthoughts.
We'd spoken a dozen times, but he can't remember my name.
"BAR—bados," he calls me, each time in the same
dactylic beat: a child attempting a new word;
a sputtering, one-wing bird.

SUMMER HEAT

Mid-morning each Saturday
(amidst the riot of rap
breakdancing from a monitor on a far wall
and washer engines whose steady call is the drone
of inter-island schooners plying citrus
in my Caribbean), I revel
among ordinary glass, ordinary metal, ordinary wood.
Behind portholes, my cottons and polyesters churn
in the foam's aggressive love.
I am midway through life's machinery
where cleanliness is next to poverty.
Outside, mid-summer heat strains against the glass
with a vertiginous grin.
But it can't catch me.

Coolly concentrated, patrons are a mosaic carnival whole:
a large mulatto sways her burdens to the gaping dryer;
an initiate twelve-year-old girl follows
with her lesser load; a prim middle-aged woman fidgets
in sheepish glances, betrays unfamiliarity
with this niche (perhaps her washer has broken today);
a bespectacled youth, smooth as sea rock,
carries his laundry bag like a carapace.
And there is patience in all but that one class-conscious eye,
the patience of another woman sitting out eleven hours
on a vessel snorting between palm-ringed shores.
All the noise, all the turbulence, and still such peace,
such calm wrapping and arranging of colours plucked
from dry mouths.

Suddenly, through the side door, a heat-wave marches
escorting a man in confederate garb.
He focuses on me,

a cross of a frown burning on his brow.
Resisting racism, I must find my weapon.
I move toward the changer and return
with a canned soda and one cool hand.
But the rest of me is on fire.

The next dryer load sears my fingertips.
Garments, like stacked half-burnt bodies, fall
to the floor and howl for Africa!
An army of flies will soon gather here
drawn by that putrid colonial breath
raging still in the Diaspora!
Cross-armed, the South's white-hot ovens
wait for me.

Once, in the loud lovely drone of engines,
in the laundered seams of poverty real as saltwater,
in the calm sorting of each carnival cloth
assembled like islands on surf,
I gloried in the shade of ordinary air.
But, please, not the heat...
I've had enough of the heat...

A CHURN IN THE SOUTH

1

"The discomfort of history, since plural man
is always discovering new ancestral ruins, is as irrevocable
as my acquired British country manners," says V.S No-Ball
flapping, southward, his flag of darkness.
I set out, from Georgia, fluttering
under that turning mincing gloom:
the words of one so full of praise
for Charleston's balustraded beauty,
he is cataracted to suburban photographs of Southerners
still *owning* their black nannies and maids.
"Strange," he ejaculates on hearing a black Charlestonian,
"tiny Barbados finding an echo
in grand South Carolina!"
Did he expect me to flip because Bajan planters
settled that city? Who gave them the wealth
to establish new lands?
The slaves, the labouring slaves.

2

A sea of trembling asphalt surrounds
a funeral home, newly painted in black and white,
the sole symbol of any equality here.
One hundred miles from Charleston,
a sign marked "ISLANDS" leaps out at me
and I think: "Home is where islands are."
Graveyards of cars, still rusting in death,
pin the sides of a highway.
My nerves are as exclamatory as pine forests
stitching the sides of a highway.
The soil changes to clay but has no meaning for me.
I hold myself in a gray place,

in self-imposed limbo, blank and neutral.
The pines that suggest my deepest fears
will crash to the ground in their time
like tons of falling roofing.
They will eat the rusty dirt of their nation,
here by man, there by hurricane.

3

I hope the double-pillared house,
to which I am headed, will contain all I need.
A brunette, swinging in a neighbouring veranda, glances
obliquely when the Celica's trunk snaps shut.
I raise a hand to her unacknowledging face,
blank as paper, pulling into itself like an anemone,
snapping into her insular sway.

A folded paper juts from my hosts' mailbox,
a white extended hyphen. It contains a key and instructions for me.
Inside, the atmosphere of children: bits
of everything everywhere. I gain my room,
the one immediately left at the top of the stairs.
A couch with no pillows. Scattered magazines, papers.
A fan at high speed whirring in its high ceiling.
I lie down and feel my body lengthen,
retaliating to this impersonal world:
the brunette anemone,
the white hyphen.

I find a chair and adjust the fan.
Even the lowest speed is too cold.
I return to the ancient couch, wondering
if it is stuffed with the hair of dead slaves.
Outside grates with electric saws
and the roar of adjacent roofing striking the ground:
the music of post-Hugo reconstruction.

Octaves below, blackbirds, like surf-circled islands, sing
for me, and I know for sure the meaning of that "ISLANDS"
sign. No-Ball's error is plain.
Islands, everywhere, regenerate; once dumb,
with new mouths they speak again.

From the balcony overlooking Charlotte Street,
that's canvassed by a blue egg-shell sky
garlanded with surfy clouds,
I see once majestic oaks (majestic as empirical kings
and queens or present-day imperial lords)
all leaf-reduced, still numbed by Hugo,
while a Gullah sea island woman carrying handmade baskets of bulrush,
sweet grass, pine needle, and palmetto,
strides homeward.

ANOTHER WAVE

Somewhere, near seawalls echoing with surf,
I re-enact the ritual of our first meeting:
every now and again your water-light lances me,
diagonally, vertically, swift impressionistic strokes.
Today, like yesterday, I laugh and cry.

With one dead eye open, one living eye closed,
I move to the giddying throb of your beauty.
Even though my memory grimaces
at the lyrically brutish waters of Cattlewash
where I saw the drowned seaman and the blood-choked sand,
like a child, I am drawn, craving to know everything.
And, like the fisherman who, despite the pound
of the sea's burgeoning claws, senses
a rare harvest, I hold my ground
tortured and hopeful as parched earth.

Meanwhile, the earth makes another turn,
and I am learning the art of waiting.
I am watching and waiting,
waiting for another wave to curve,
for the riptide's cunning to be finally exposed
so I can swim again, a solitary man but happier than most,
along the blue-ribboned legs of the coast.

TWO PAINTINGS

(for Malaika Favorite)

1

Two men, one woman, emaciated, throatless
in the cloudy eye of nature.
Between bald heads and levitating graduation caps,
a river of space. A scholastic god's blue finger
forks its blessings down in thunder claps.
The bespectacled man has waited all his life for this.
So, too, the woman, legs crossed in bliss.
Each one looks a separate way.
Only the second man realises his cap is gone,
but the stasis and frowning shoulder betray
his own bondage in the cuff of an unseen hand.
Like the rest, he's allowed himself to submit
to abstraction and is lost. Not even Miss America's kiss
can revive him now. His submission
reeks of the kind one makes to a politician
who promises gold to all believers. In the gaping
spaces between these three, clouds are rivering
romancing the lost with clenched fists.

2

Through a window, a woman's hand reaches down
and coalesces with variegated immortelles
sprouting bottom left of this world.
Her almond-brown eyes devour the harbourscape a mile away.
An hour earlier, her mother left for the waterside, with the man,
but she couldn't bear it.
"Every time he leave,
something like a dagger does turn
real slow inside me.

I hear de sea say:
'Seaman, is time to go again,
time to ride your other woman'."

A dried immortelle's leaf propellers to the ground.
For no reason (save the woman's jealous thoughts)
the sea sweeps over the world,
then quietens, laughs, toying
with the separateness of men and women.

SOMEWHERE, SOMEWHERE

Rain, a faithful hangman, this morning tapped
my hazy window pane:
the slow pounding of a trapped
dove. Somehow, I just can't escape this rain.

Here, as elsewhere, a caged sun follows me.
I'm stuck to her face like Van Gogh's oils,
my mania, my mania, a howling sea.
Toward my gnarled lips, Love's acrid gunsmoke coils.

Rain of erasure, galling rain,
hangs a song, breaks a song, makes and dies.
And when I go down to-low-town-low-town-low-town,
my bones will sound their melody.

Here by my window, I recall the making of a new road.
I hear a crow's shrilled
beseeching as the falling load
of marl buries one wing. The other cannot be stilled.

I open the window. Rain, the hangman, covers
me, extends the borders of his garment
over me. My cupped hands shrink: uncertain lovers
wings bleeding   separate   silent.

HOTEL POOLSIDE

Under a blue-bell umbrella sprouting
from a round marble table, I sip
lemon squash with chipped ice
to ease my chronic dryness.
Not far in front me, an amniotic sea swells.

A woman, like striding mahogany,
reaches the poolside. With Nefertiti's careful grace,
she disrobes to a blue bikini
and coils in a lounger next to me.
A shirtless, hairy-chested man strolls around the pool.
Gently and firmly, he drums on a guitar's thigh, strums,
defies this Paradise's lyric law:

> *Bajan politicians are heartless,*
> *and if you ask me if I mean that, I do.*
> *They kill their artists.*
> *The drawn blades come for true.*

A waiter hovers
and I, encouraged, order two rums:
one for me, one for my new neighbour.
Our glasses kiss awkwardly, and we titter.

"Last year in Mexico," she says,
"my husband left for his last scuba dive,
defying a bad heart and the doctor's advice."
She sighs as if she would wrench all tanks
from the back of the world.
Like me, parched with many hurts,
dry with rejection, trying to forget.
Drawn by that common tide,
memory tightening, I grip the lounger's side.
My lust quivers out to sea,
too confounded, too hungry to rise.

AIRPORT REVISITED

An emergency light flashed like a fear.
The Captain said, "We must return to Barbados."
Our agitated breaths scurried down the aisle

in his direction wondering: why us?
We had just sliced a rainbow
and cheered for life.

"Please remain seated, calm. This'll take just a little while."
His voice was surer, a baritone. Our restless palms didn't dry,
and our minds reeled with images of an *Airport*:

a plane scalps the sea, then floats on top like a dead
fish. Water rolls at its windows.
Our souls sink like weights into the spheres,

tossed and bruised. The plane strikes the seabed.
Our hysteria pierces the half-lit cabin.
A doctor bends over three small children.

Through a window crack, water trickles like our tears.
A mother stabs the Captain with blame. If those windows pop,
who will help us out? Who lift us up?

In the adjacent row, wrapped with worry,
a girl wailed. If we'd fallen, what to do but bless
friends and family, pray and go loudly to a watery rest?

Through my window, I saw the island greenery
swim into view. It floated
on the sea's blue couch: a green pillow

hand-embroidered, stuffed with love.
My eyes fastened there and wouldn't move.
We landed. "Just a faulty light," the Captain said.

A DANCER TO THE GODS

1

The 747 lifts as smoothly as those parakeets
perpetually changing guard along pages of yellow sand;
as smooth but not as silent.
Its roar has little in common with saltwater kingdoms.
Its metal reeks of urbanity, of a life
equal to its speed, where reflection can be a luxury
and, if uncultivated, can make the spirit buckle and sag.
The straits of memory are all one has to bridge the gap
between north and south
between past-present and future-present
between the gnarled skyscraper and the water's edge.

Even as the trundling legs vanish inside the grating stomach,
and the island's rugged eastern shoulder
looms and, as suddenly, disappears,
tears stream diagonally across the plane's window.
Tonya's tears. She misses me now as she dresses
for school at seven forty-five a.m.
When I disembark, I too will be in school,
I too will shout a loud amen
and earn my keep in this northern state,
three thousand miles from where they left me,
tortured and rejected, to rot
on golden beaches.

All movement of water is elastic: diagonals,
cubes, horizontals, verticals,
all converge on me.
Salt
from the water made to drown me
heals my wounds.
I am blindfolded, banished.

In the roar of that exclusion, in the abyss
of spite and bad-mindedness,
I soar on the back of a giant parakeet.
I hug and kiss the sun
which none can take from me.

2

I have perfected a Creole art:
the complex singularity of twin horizons.
Aurora and Evilynn, two forks of a sling shot
(past-present/future-present)
and I the hurled rock, some say spoilt,
lovely in pain.
Now, I am poised but, like the wind,
I could change again.
This black rock could return to Aurora Beach
and be based exclusively in surf;
it could invite narrow-minded Aurora to fly
with it to faraway places;
or it could remain in exile on Evilynn Avenue
gutted with white azaleas and the royal oak
and there make love to this mistress to the god of surf.
I dance wherever there is good music.
Today, I grabble, then slowly caress
a piece of this foreign earth
bursting with the music of pink azaleas
and the wisteria's mauve perfume:
my harvest, my mistress, my blind love.

3

I eat a slice of Venezuela's hefty beefy shoulder
and then the toasted islands: Bonaire, Aruba, Curaçao.
At thirty-one thousand feet, the ocean's rifled with clouds,
the sky, asterisked with palms — a parallax paradise.

How can I be contented to love one shore, one space,
in the wake of such variety?
Each asterisk is a highlight in the scheme of things.
That Jewish gent surrounded by the vacuity of the Bronx,
is as much an islander as the man playing cricket
on an almond-ringed beach in Barbados!

Year-round, carnival rocks encircle themselves
with turquoise bandages. Sometimes they smell
and must be changed. Those bandages mask
the foot of the dead, year round.

Take Haiti: the bulging land mass twists and heaves
like flesh in a horror movie. It rises hopelessly
with every wasted election. A people's hand
is permanently outstretched, palms facing upward
to a voodoo god drained of answers.
One outstretched hand falls.
Another will fall in the morning.
The hills smoke endlessly like burning pyres.
I speak as layman to the land.
I sing as gut response to islands
choked and cluttered with partisan voices.
I am blue with disappointment
but green with thanksgiving: my parakeet
wings me to the banks of space,
into orange hearts of island sunsets,
over the lake of the Caribbean Sea
in which stratified men and women
can see themselves, can see
the bride and the groom in themselves
emerging fresh and whole
on their morning of cloud
on their morning of palm
on their morning of surf.

THE LONG GAP

Over half my life ago, I walked on this linkage of tar
with Everton, whom we called "Cat Face", and Cameron
who laughed at everything. The distance seemed far,
so far that often we'd break into a run
if we felt we'd be late for school or home.
We were shorter then, our visions small.

Nearing middle-age, I disembark from a mini-bus,
named "Not Guilty, Your Honour", where Spooner's Hill
meets Long Gap in a carnival of heat. Mid-afternoon sun
blares like too-loud dub music. It tries to kill
my reverie of six ixoras, blaring softly in red,
that, an hour ago, I placed
by mum's grave-head in Sharon Church's yard.
Is this why poetry doesn't come easy here? The noise?
The noise of the sun? Noise of the unemployed? Noise
of the mini-buses stampeding like hell?

I must never let down my guard.
I force my mind on the six ixoras,
on the labelled honey jar I put them in
half-filled with pure island water,
on how I scoop-out a hole in front the gravestone
and fixed the jar in its miniature mound.
A faint breeze blows thanksgiving from my mouth.
Five red and yellow butterflies fly out from the grave.
I keep these. I keep these for Tonya who I'm on my way to see
in the innocent classroom of Grazettes Primary.

My feet revise this asphalt's history.
Brick houses, trees, the road itself, all seem
to contract, crowd in urgent neuroses — a material bacchanal.
What happened to Mackie Downes' house with its gentle yellows

and the decorative guard walls on which we used to sit
during elementary days? Where is John Browne's, brown
like him and high in the air? Where is Mackie?
Where is John? Where is John's sister, the one
who made fire roar in my belly? Where her neighbour,
the wing-thrilling Ann, to whom, it was said, I gave
one of my high school athletic trophies?
(I never did. I have all nine of them).
Up ahead, Roach's shop projects its signs
like a hooker's breasts: coke, ju-c, banks beer.
The sun glazes nearby canefields with benign
indifference. If the quarry is still there, it will yawn
like a half-asleep drunk in the shop's back room and slink
under the oppression of the heat.

Inside, I order the coldest soda. A fear
of familiarity consumes me. Miss Roach shows no hint
of recognition. Anonymity has its blessings. I can think
without the distraction of how-you-do. The pungency
of salted-cod barrels invades my nostrils.
Full-breasted still but greying now, the shopkeeper talks
in gutturals to a man in a straw hat
leaned against the counter.
They look around at me. Her eyes tear
open. Recognition crams the air!
Her head jerks from my gaze. My insides, a swirling sea.
Does she remember the summer
Mackie and I stole her sugar cane?
Will she call the police?
Outside, the furnaces enfold me again.
I move through part of the Government-owned housing area.
Looking up, my eyes tremble into Catface's
upstairs window and its faded cream curtains.
I hear he is somewhere in the States, just like me.
Where? I don't know.

On the ground floor of the next block, a black man
and his Indian common-law wife would liven the place
with their parties. All the women
screwed their brows and flashed and fastened their eyes
until the Trini lady invited them all
and won affection through their growling guts.
She was short, plumpish; her lipstick, flamboyant red;
her body, a ripe pear, arousing, firm...

The landing scheme spreads wide its chattel and brick arms
on a single level. The Government-owned land still bristles
with homeowners' pride. My father brought his two-bedroom chattel
from Whitehall and placed it here
until neighbourhood vices threatened to crush his skull
and steal his "breathing space".
It comes too fast, this tryst with origins.
Too fast the shocking decay and the mind's wrestling
with what was and now is:
a remnant of paint peels like dried mahogany bark.
The walkway seems to violently contract.
I cannot even sprint along it anymore.
Seven marble holes punctuated that track.
The Lady of the Night arced and sentried this entrance.
Two beds of variegated crotons, hibiscus, and Pride
of Barbados half-hugged the place. Now,
an emaciated walkway empty of life.

The stranger comes to the side window and cannot let me in.
She alone and you don't know who is who nowadays.
I ask if the Greens still live next door and how about
the Spooners and Miss Thompson at the corner of the road
and Honey next door, the blackest woman I ever knew, black
until she shone. I sound for real so she feelings change.
The rusted galvanised gate creaks in inches
to allow my head's entrance and the cacophonous welcome
of indignant budgerigars railing in cages from the centre.

Once, Henry's pigeon coup stood in that contentious spot.
Now the step and the cellar miniaturise to my want,
but the coconut and banana trees have been eaten by grime.

I break toward Grazettes Primary.
I pass the house of the tall bald-headed "Donut Man"
whose floury circles we devoured each day.
O and he had a daughter and I did want to hold she hand
but was too terrified by the strangest feelings
that butchered my voice. Years later,
I saw her shopping tall in Bridgetown,
clothed in Iman's lolling loveliness,
and my limbs went slack with lust.
Our eyes recognised. They somersaulted like waves,
but our mouths said nothing.

At fifteen, we moved to Brittons Hill
to "get more breathing space". Angela fled
to England seven years before. So the mother
and four males, Dad, Henry, Winston, and me, hoisted
the two-bedroomed chattel on to the back of a truck,
and something in me was lost forever.
I left friends I never found again.
I wrestle with an angel from that past:
Dawn comes laden with dew.
I'm running around "The Square",
slamming dominoes under the moth-fluttering street light
by Miss Browne's shop,
exploring island caves all summer long
and the shimmering tourist-laden beaches.
In the gathering dark, we take up our clothes
from off crab-filled rocks
while, behind us, ripples wash and breakers softly roar.
Many of us are here: Henry and Winston;
the Grazettes: Valance, Orrie, John, Phonso, and Clyde;
the Leaches: Tony, Trevor, Austin; Charles and Gordon;

the Untouchables: Sink the Schooner (or Cynthia),
Avril, Pinkie, Annette, Pauline; the bride-
like, hop-scotching Janis, whose cheeks I once touched
under the streetlight;
and Lynnette who lived next to Mr. Ross
the retired civil servant
with the first T.V in our district.
We ran around "The Square" in the evening.
We slammed dominoes under the streetlight
until that western theme spiralled uphill
like gunsmoke: "*Bonanza*, Boys!!" we bellowed.
Mr. Ross's face set like concrete at our stampede.
Yet, the door faithfully cracked its six inches.
We crammed each vacant space. As the stars increased
like domino dots, we inched inside
and found seats on the carpeted floor.
Behind his gorgon stare, a widower's lonely heart danced.

O something in me ruptured.
To go back, to go back
to clutch the roots of the word
to stay and hope for the suspension to snap
to grab the baton from the past's cliff-edge.
Not to leave with the song only part sung
not to leave without saying goodbye.
I am not afraid to go back, go back,
not scared to rouse the fire of leaving,
unresolved memory; not afraid to grab
the cliff-edge of the past
even though it may be too late.
Too late, Janis, whose velvet cheek
I touched when I was thirteen.
After a ten-year interlude of dream,
we sat under a coconut tree in Brittons Hill
healing each other with words:
My dad drowned at Cattlewash,

your children's father giving you horrors.
You married him still,
and my spirit fled into the dark.
Next year, your marriage struck a reef
while another's ring encircled me.
We never touched the hot crest of the wave.
Too late, Janis of my high-school diaries,
too late the dream that never knew flesh.
The rehearsals are infinite.
I saw you last at a basketball
game at the Y, out of shape,
and soured by the hardness of life.

So dad died with the sea in his flesh.
Angela, unprepared and deaf to advice,
swapped England for Africa.
The twin exile drove her through sun and rain
to her true wing fleshed in coral.
But she never saw her two boychildren again.
And Henry, hounded by some mysterious ghost
(he was doing so well here in the island),
fled north to feel for himself
England's cold sunshine.
He glances back once, a meteor's glance.
The gap has grown too long.
Neither the rum, sun and calypso,
nor the white mother of the north can excite him.
His phosphorescence burns, then quickly disappears.
Mother, bearer of all things,
lover of all things,
calmly expires at seventy-six
her spirit hoisting an image:
Angela, cancerous vines prowling through her,
dead at forty-three.
And Winston holds a brush in his hand.
He stands before an easel painting words.

Pictures and words. These two
are left.

Yes, I come from Sharon   just now
from the life of the graveyard   just now
to the brink of the school yard   just now
and Tonya comes running
with a lunch-box in her hand
and a back-pack on her shoulders
and I run and hug her   just now
and she smile-up in my face   just now
I say: "Everything will be all right just now"
and I look on the sunlight   just now

GLOSSARY

Bussa. Slave leader of Barbados' 1816 revolt, the largest in the island. A statue, that captures his spirit, points toward St. George, the island's most central parish.

castle's legs. A reference to Sam Lord's Castle (on the island's south eastern coast) named after the notorious English pirate who lured ships onto the reefs by lanterns hung in coconut trees. Sam Lord's Castle is now a hotel.

CBC. The Caribbean Broadcasting Corporation in Barbados.

Clement Payne. Mobiliser of the Barbadian working class during the 1937 revolt against the plantocracy.

Gullah. African-descended peoples who inhabit a group of islands off the South Carolina coast.

Hugo. Hurricane of 1989 which devastated the city of Charleston, South Carolina.

ixora. Blood-red tropical flower.

moses. A small light fishing boat.

Nefertiti. An ancient Egyptian queen whose husband, King Akhenaton, ruled from 1367 to 1350 B.C.

Nelson. Admiral Lord Nelson, British naval war hero whose statue stands at Trafalgar Square in Bridgetown, the capital of Barbados.

paling. Common wall-like yard enclosure of the Caribbean of corrugated galvanised sheets normally five to seven feet high.

rukatuk. Music of the Barbados Tuk bands.

shakshak. Dark flat long pod of the flamboyant tree.

Tom Adams. A former Prime Minister of Barbados who died suddenly and mysteriously in 1985, two years after the U.S. led invasion of Grenada. Barbados played a central role during the invasion, allowing the U.S. use of its airport for transhipment purposes.

Anthony Kellman was born in Barbados and educated there and in the U.S., where he is a professor of English and creative writing at Augusta State University, Georgia. He is the author of another book of poetry, *Watercourse* (1990) and a novel, *The Coral Rooms* (1994) both published by Peepal Tree. In 1992, he edited the first full-length U.S. anthology of English-speaking Caribbean poetry, *Crossing Water*. A recipient of a National Endowment for the Arts fellowship, his poetry, fiction, and critical essays have appeared in periodicals and anthologies in the Commonwealth and the U.S.